POLAR BEARS, PENGUINS,
AND OTHER MYSTERIOUS ANIMALS OF THE
EXTREME COLD

ANA MARÍA RODRÍGUEZ

Enslow Publishers, Inc.
40 Industrial Road
Box 398
Berkeley Heights, NJ 07922
USA

http://www.enslow.com

For my husband and sons, who share my journeys through extreme worlds

Acknowledgments

The author expresses her immense gratitude to the scientists who so kindly gave their time to comment on the manuscript and provided images to illustrate the book. Your help has been extremely invaluable.

Library of Congress Cataloging-in-Publication Data

Rodriguez, Ana Maria, 1958–
  Polar bears, penguins, and other mysterious animals of the extreme cold / Ana María Rodríguez.
    p. cm. — (Extreme animals in extreme environments)
  Includes bibliographical references and index.
  Summary: "Explains why the Arctic and Antarctic are extreme environments and examines how polar bears, penguins, and other animals have adapted to the cold"—Provided by publisher.
  ISBN 978-0-7660-3695-6
  1. Animals—Polar regions—Juvenile literature. 2. Polar regions—Juvenile literature. I. Title.
  QL104.R63 2011
  591.70911—dc22
                                2010015678

Paperback ISBN 978-1-4644-0017-9
ePUB ISBN 978-1-4645-0467-9
PDF ISBN 978-1-4646-0467-6

Printed in the United States of America

092011 Lake Book Manufacturing, Inc., Melrose Park, IL

10 9 8 7 6 5 4 3 2 1

Illustration Credits: Andrew Derocher, University of Alberta, pp. 16, 17; British Antarctic Survey, p. 36; Carlie Reum / National Science Foundation, p. 40; D. J. Jennings / National Science Foundation, p. 30; Donna Naughton / Canadian Museum of Nature, p. 15; Emily Stone / National Science Foundation, p. 33; Glenn Grant / National Science Foundation, p. 34; Katy Jensen / National Science Foundation, p. 27; Melanie Conner / National Science Foundation, p. 8; Mike Usher / National Science Foundation, p. 28; © 2011 Photos. com, a division of Getty Images, pp. 4, 7, 9, 10, 13, 18, 21, 25, 39; Shutterstock.com, pp. 1, 3; Zina Deretsky / National Science Foundation, p. 41.

Cover Illustration: Shutterstock.com (Polar Bear).

CONTENTS

"Cold, terrible cold:
At -50°C a flashlight dies in his hand;
at -55°C kerosene freezes;
at -60°C rubber turns brittle and snaps . . ."[1]

—Robert Burleigh, from *Black Whiteness*, 1998

1
THE ICY WORLDS:
THE ARCTIC AND ANTARCTICA

The Arctic and Antarctica are two of the most extreme environments in the world. The Arctic is located at the northernmost region of the world, while Antarctica is on the southernmost region of Earth. The North Pole is located in the Arctic Ocean and the South Pole is in Antarctica.

They are freezing cold, frostbite windy, lip-cracking dry, and pitch-black for half of the year. Despite these extreme conditions, many magnificent animals call these icy worlds home.

Polar bears, penguins, whales, seals, arctic foxes, rabbits, a myriad of insects, birds, fish, plants, and microbes are some of the creatures that live in the icy worlds. Most people, however, would have a hard time surviving there. How do animals do it?

AMAZING ANTARCTICA

✳ **The coldest air temperature recorded so far is -132° Fahrenheit (-91°Celsius) at the Vostok Russian research station, Antarctica, in 1997.[2]**

✳ **Antarctica is also the driest place, receiving no precipitation at all for months in a year.[3]**

✳ **The fastest winds ever recorded roared over Antarctica in 1972.[4] They traveled at 200 miles per hour (322 kilometers per hour), which is faster than catastrophic Category 5 hurricanes.**

✳ **Antarctica is the highest continent. It rises 1.4 miles (2.2 kilometers) above the sea.[5]**

Scientists have been amazed and curious about how animals survive in such extremely cold places with limited food. To find out, they have been traveling to the icy worlds to study these extreme animals. Their hard work has revealed amazing animal adaptations.

LIFE IN THE ICY WORLDS

Many types of animals live in the icy worlds. However, not many live there permanently. Some animals migrate to warmer lands during the winter and return during summer. They avoid the most extreme conditions they are not adapted to survive in. Many migratory birds, such as geese, and mammals, such as caribou, use this strategy.

Other animals hibernate in an underground shelter to avoid the freezing weather and the lack of food. Hibernating is a deep sleeplike state during which the animal's

The arctic fox, like the polar bear, spends its life in the Arctic.
Its white fur helps it blend into its surroundings.

body functions slow down. The body temperature drops, and the animal does not need to eat or even defecate. It is warmer inside the underground shelter than it is outside. This helps animals not to freeze. The ground squirrel hibernates in the Arctic.[6]

MASTERS OF THE ICY WORLDS

The most extreme animals of the Arctic and Antarctica live there permanently and stay active. The masters of the icy worlds are the polar bear, a mammal of the Arctic, and the emperor penguin, a bird of Antarctica.

The polar bear and the emperor penguin are successful because they stay warm, find enough food, and have babies under conditions many other animals find deadly. One key reason for their success is that both are endotherms, or warm-blooded.

The Antarctic cod does not freeze thanks to antifreeze proteins in its blood.

WHY ARE THE ICY WORLDS EXTREMELY COLD?

1. They receive a fraction of the solar energy other parts of the world receive because the Earth is tilted as it revolves around the sun.[7]

2. White snow and ice reflect, or bounce back, about 85 percent of the solar energy they receive. This is the albedo effect. Darker ground, on the other hand, absorbs a larger amount of solar energy that warms it up.[8]

3. For about half of the year, there is more darkness than light. At the poles, it is daylight for six months during summer, and it is dark during winter.

4. It can get very windy. Fast winds cause a wind chill effect, which drops temperatures significantly. A temperature of -40°F (-40°C) will feel like -86°F (-65°C) if the wind is blowing at 45 mph (72 kmh).[9] Antarctica is the windiest place on Earth.

The amazing icy landscape of Antarctica.

Reindeer migrate south of the Arctic in the winter and return in the spring.

Like all other mammals and birds, polar bears and emperor penguins maintain their body temperature with the heat produced by their body or metabolism. Their body temperature remains the same regardless of how cold it gets. This is the opposite of ectotherms, or cold-blooded animals, whose body temperature is determined by the environment. Reptiles, insects, amphibians, and fish are ectotherms. When it gets extremely cold, ectotherms cannot keep their bodies warm enough to move around to find food. They must leave for a warmer place, enter hibernation, or have another adaptation to survive.

Read on and discover where polar bears and emperor penguins come from. How did they end up living in extremely cold environments? And how did they become the masters of the icy worlds?

2
THE POLAR BEAR:
THE ICE MASTER OF THE ARCTIC

More than 200,000 years ago, there were no polar bears on Earth. Polar bears are related to brown bears that ventured into the Arctic during the ice age called the Pleistocene. To survive in this extreme environment, the ancestors of the polar bear changed some of their physical characteristics and habits over a long period of time.[1]

FACING A TOUGH CHALLENGE

Thousands of years ago brown bears living on the Arctic mainland, from Siberia to Nunavut in Canada, explored northern territories looking for food. During winter, the bears could move back to warmer southern lands.

The Pleistocene age occurred between 2 million and ten thousand years ago.

The polar bear's ancestor probably looked a lot like this grizzly bear. Grizzly bears are a subspecies of the brown bear.

DO BEARS HIBERNATE?

Hibernating animals spend the winter in a dormant state. Some animals, such as hedgehogs, are deep hibernators. They drop their body temperature close to the freezing point of water (32°F or 0°C). They slow down their heartbeat and their breathing. They are slow to wake up when disturbed. Bears are not deep hibernators. They appear to be sleeping deeply, but they wake up quickly if disturbed. Their body temperature drops a little. Their breathing and heartbeat slow down, but not as much as deep hibernators.[2]

Probably most kept up their normal winter "hibernation." They remained inside dens when it was too cold or food was scarce until the weather warmed up and food became more abundant.[3]

The ancestors of the polar bear found the food they liked in these northern lands. Being omnivores, they ate both plants and animals. They dug out roots, licked insects from rotting wood, or gorged on wild berries. They pulled small animals like ground squirrels out of their burrows, or hunted moose or caribou. They even ate carrion or rotting flesh from a dead animal.[4]

But this was the Ice Age. It became so cold that ice covered large areas of the ocean. Ice sheets grew very large on the mainland forming glaciers that blocked the path to warmer, southern lands. The polar bear ancestors became isolated in a frozen world.[5]

Polar bear ancestors had to adapt "quickly" if they were going to survive. The polar bear split off from its brown bear ancestors 150,000 years ago. It may not seem "quick," but compared to other species that take millions of years to become what we see today, the polar bear developed much faster.

During all those years, polar bears developed distinctive characteristics and behaviors that allow them to be the masters of their icy realm. These characteristics and behaviors allow them to survive—to avoid freezing, find enough food, and have cubs.

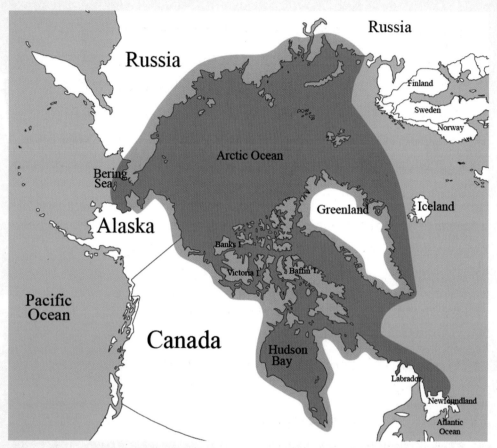

The colored area in this map shows where polar bears live. They have not been seen in the white areas of the map.

THE NEED TO STAY WARM

The polar bear ancestors that survived in the Arctic developed an amazing insulation. Insulation is a material that prevents or reduces heat loss. Polar bears stay warm thanks to dense fur made of two layers—long guard hairs and short, thicker underwool.

Fur works well because it traps air in the spaces between hairs. Air conducts heat poorly. It does not let the heat from the bear's skin to escape to the freezing environment surrounding the bear. Also, fur covers most of their body, even most of the bottom of their paws. Very little surface remains uncovered through which they could lose heat. Only their black nose and foot pads are fur-free. Brown bears do not have fur as thick as that of polar bears.

A scientist measures the large paw of a polar bear. Thick fur surrounds the paw pads.

Polar bears are the largest carnivores on land (and ice). Dr. Andrew Derocher has put a polar bear to sleep for a few hours so he can measure him.

Dry fur insulates bears well. Wet fur, however, does not keep bears warm because it loses the air trapped between the hairs. Think of how useless a wet jacket is. Nevertheless, polar bears do not get cold when they swim in the freezing Arctic Sea. They have a thick layer of fat under their skin that is also good insulation.

Their ears and tail are small and furry, allowing less heat loss than larger ones. Polar bears have become the largest bears alive and the largest land carnivore (although they spend most of the time on ice or in the water). Having a large body also helps keep the body warm.[6]

CHANGING THE MENU

Finding food is imperative, too. Polar bears prefer to eat seals, especially ringed seals. When polar bear ancestors arrived in the Arctic hundreds of thousands of years ago, seals were already living in the Arctic Ocean. They were abundant and widespread when other sources of food were not easy to find. So polar bear ancestors gradually changed their menu toward a mainly carnivorous diet.

They learned to hunt seals and other aquatic mammals in the pack ice—frozen seawater. The pack ice provided a platform for the bears to catch seals, which make for a rich meal.[7] Polar bears eat mainly the blubber and the skin of seals, the parts that give them the most energy.

Polar bears are powerful hunters. Notice its long canine teeth, specially adapted to tear into prey.

They often leave the flesh for other arctic residents, such as arctic foxes and ravens. Polar bear canine teeth, or fangs, are larger and sharper than those of brown bears. Large, sharp canines are the trademark of carnivorous mammals.

SKILLED HUNTERS

To catch seals, polar bears became expert hunters. Polar bears wear the perfect outfit, or camouflage, for hunting in the pack ice—white fur. Because polar bear hairs are transparent and hollow, they reflect light making them look white. Seals resting on the pack ice cannot spot white bears easily against the white background.

Polar bears are also good hunters because they have an excellent sense of smell. They can even smell a seal pup hidden inside an ice den covered by 3 feet (1 meter) of snow from a mile away!

Polar bears combine a few hunting techniques. They sniff out a pup in an ice den beneath the sea ice, break into the den, and catch the pup. A polar bear will pound the icy den with its front paws powered with its body weight (average weight is 780–1,500 pounds, or 352–680 kilograms). Finally, the icy cover breaks exposing a helpless seal pup.

Polar bears became patient hunters. Sometimes they wait for hours until adult seals rise to the surface of their breathing holes, called aglus. The bear may lie down by the breathing hole, knowing that sooner or later a seal will rise to breathe. As soon as the bear hears the seal blowing air as it emerges, the bear will smash its head with a plate-sized paw. It then pulls the seal out of the water with its sharp, non-retractable 2-inch-long (5-centimeter-long) claws, where it cannot escape. Occasionally, polar bears that lose a seal after a long period of waiting will show signs of frustration.[8]

A MARINE MAMMAL

The polar bears' ancestors were land mammals, but polar bears became marine mammals. Their scientific name, *Ursus maritimus,* means "sea bear." They are of the sea because they depend almost completely on food from the sea. They also spend most of their lives either on pack ice—frozen seawater—or swimming.

Polar bears are very good swimmers. They can swim for several hours at a time and cover long distances. Some bears have been tracked swimming for 62 miles (100 kilometers). This is useful when they want to reach ice floes on which seals or walruses gather. Sometimes, polar bears stalk their prey from the water and jump to the ice to catch them by surprise. This is another example of their intelligence and great strength.[9]

A few characteristics make polar bears well adapted to the sea. For example, their teardrop-shaped bodies help them swim easily. They have webbed paws, which also help them to swim faster while their hind legs work as a rudder. They are also good divers. They can hold their breath a few minutes and keep their eyes open and the nostrils closed underwater.

Polar bears are excellent swimmers. Mothers teach their young how to navigate the freezing waters of the Arctic.

CHANGING SLEEPING HABITS

Brown bears sleep in dens on land during the winter when food is scarce. But the polar bear ancestors trying to survive in the frozen Arctic found abundant food in the winter: seals. Today, except for denning females, many polar bears, especially adult males, do not sleep out the winter. They spend it actively hunting seals.[10]

During winter, the pack ice reaches its maximum extent and thickness. Leads, which are long stretches of open water enclosed by ice, and breathing holes remain open in winter. They allow access to

A THREATENED SPECIES

In May 2008, the U.S. Department of the Interior declared the polar bear threatened under the Endangered Species Act.[11] The polar bear is threatened because the Arctic pack ice is decreasing. Because polar bears depend on the pack ice for their survival, a slow but progressive reduction of the summer pack ice is a threat to the 20,000 to 25,000 polar bears living in the Arctic.

ringed seals, who spend most of their lives in the pack ice. The pack ice is where polar bears spend most of their time looking for food.

Polar bears stay active during spring because that is when seal pups are born. Polar bears hunt them intensely, packing on fat reserves. This will help them survive summer and fall seasons when the pack ice retreats, and they have less access to the seals.

EXPECTING CUBS

To survive in the Arctic, polar bear ancestors adapted their way of having cubs. Females usually get pregnant during the spring, sometime between April and May. However, the embryos do not grow until the beginning of the winter. It is like they place the cub's development on hold until the mother has stored enough fat—energy—for a safe pregnancy in mid-winter. Also, it is not until winter that enough snow accumulates for the mother polar bear to dig a den.

UNDER THE SNOW

Mother bears adapted to the Arctic by building dens under thick snow instead of using caves or other land dens like brown bears. The mother bear's dwelling usually has one chamber the size of a large closet, but not as tall. The chamber connects to the surface through a tunnel whose entrance is usually lower than the chamber. This acts as a trap for body heat, like an Inuk igloo.

A thick layer of snow insulates the chamber from the outside. Fluffy snow traps air inside, and it provides good insulation. The temperature inside the den is about 32°F (0°C), which is higher than the outside temperature, which may be as low as -58°F (-50°C). This provides a stable environment for the new cubs.[12]

SLEEPING IT OFF

While in the den, the mother bear does not eat, drink, or defecate. Like other types of bears, she doesn't enter deep hibernation. She reduces her activity to survive on the fat reserves she accumulated during summer, fall, and early winter. Her body temperature drops slightly around 95°F (35°C), or it may remain normal at 98.6 °F (37°C). Her breathing slows down to about three times per minute. Her heart beats slower, from 70 to 8 beats per minute.[13] She appears to be sleeping deeply but wakes up easily if disturbed by anything. She spends about three months doing little more than resting and feeding her cubs.

RICH MILK FOR GROWING FAST

The cubs are born in the middle of the Arctic winter. The mother may have one, two, or three cubs but usually two. They are small, weighing about 1.5 pounds (0.7 kilograms). They are blind and do not have a layer of fat and a thick fur coat to protect them from the cold, yet. So they stay inside the den with their mother. She keeps them warm with her body and feeds them very rich milk.

Thirty-one percent of the milk is fat and 10 percent is protein—similar to the composition of seal and whale milk. For comparison, human milk is 4 percent fat. The cubs grow quickly on this highly nutritious diet. They have grown to about 25 pounds (12 kilograms) when they leave the den in the spring.[14]

When the mother and cubs emerge from the den in spring, the mother slowly gets the cubs used to the outside world. She shows them how to feed themselves as she looks for food to replenish the fat reserves she had lost while fasting and feeding her young inside the den. The cubs stay with their mother for about two years. In this time, they must learn how to hunt and to relate with other bears to survive.

During thousands of years, the extreme icy world of the Arctic shaped many generations of polar bear ancestors. What we see today is one of the best-adapted creatures of the world: a first-rate carnivore at the top of the Arctic food chain.

A mother polar bear nurses her two cubs.

3
THE EMPEROR PENGUIN:
THE MOST EXTREME PENGUIN OF ANTARCTICA

A long, long time ago, more than 60 million years ago, in a time called the Paleocene, there were no penguins on Earth. But the penguins' ancestors were already flying the skies. They were probably a type of diving bird similar to today's albatross or diving petrels.[1] How did a flying bird that lived in a warm place become a flightless bird that only lives in the coldest place on Earth?

A CHANGING LAND

Sixty million years ago, Antarctica was a tropical land covered with forests. The temperatures were warmer on land and in the ocean. This is where the oldest ancestors of penguins began their history.

Sixty million years ago, Antarctica was not located at the South Pole but between the equator and the South Pole. All the continents drift and change their positions in time. And so did Antarctica. In time, it moved to the South Pole. (The continents continue moving today).

During this period, the climate became much colder. The sea surface surrounding Antarctica froze, and snow piled up for years on land and never melted. Permanent ice was the new landscape. There was no more open ground with trees, bushes, or even rocks available to build a nest. These changes occurred over a very long time.

A scientist measures the bill length of a giant petrel chick at Palmer Station in the western part of the Antarctic Peninsula. The penguins' ancestors may have been similar to today's petrels.

Penguin ancestors faced a tremendous challenge and responded in different ways. Some penguins moved north where it was not as cold as in Antarctica. Today, penguins can be found up to the equator. Some penguins could not adapt and perished. Emperor penguins adapted to an icy world with extremely cold weather. Of the seventeen species of penguins living today, only the emperor penguin spends all year long in Antarctica.

King penguins look very similar to emperor penguins, but they are smaller and live on islands north of Antarctica. Elephant seals are the largest seals in the world.

IT IS ALL IN THE NAME

The emperor penguin's scientific name is *Aptenodytes forsteri.* *Aptenodytes* means "featherless diver."[2]

THE LIFE OF THE EMPEROR PENGUIN

It is not easy living in Antarctica all year long. Just like the polar bear in the Arctic, emperor penguins thrive in Antarctica because they have adapted to avoid freezing, to find enough food, and raise their chicks. They combine amazing physical characteristics with an incredible journey that begins with a good meal.

MARCH: TIME TO FEAST

In March, which is summer season in Antarctica, emperor penguins spend many days diving and gobbling up huge amounts of fish and squid. They gain a lot of weight by building fat reserves, which will be very useful later. Some males may double the weight they had at the end of winter.[3]

To survive in Antarctica, emperor penguin ancestors had to stay warm. They achieved that thanks to several adaptations. Two of them are a thick layer of blubber and a dense coat of tightly packed water-proof feathers.

Penguins in Petermann Island, Antarctic Peninsula. Notice the large brown guano stains on the ice. Guano is another name for penguin droppings.

BLUBBER AND FEATHERS

A layer of blubber under the skin is a very good insulator. It transfers heat poorly from the warm penguin's body to the cold water around it. Blubber is also a good insulator on land and on the ice, even when facing a blizzard.

The second adaptation is their coat of feathers. They have about seventy feathers in one square inch (6.5 square centimeters) of their body, which is more than that of any other bird. The short outer feathers overlap, like tiles on a roof, to form a thick waterproof layer. There are almost no spaces between each feather through which water may seep in and chill the body. Underneath, fluffier feathers keep the penguins warm by trapping air among them.

Preening oil, which is a waxy, water-repellent substance, coats the feathers and keeps them waterproof. A gland at the base of the tail produces the oil. Penguins preen or spread this substance on the feathers with their beaks. Preening also realigns the feathers to keep them tightly packed.[4]

BIG AND TALL, FOR A PENGUIN

Emperor penguins are the largest of all penguins. They are about 3.8 feet (1.15 meters) tall and weigh about 88 pounds (40 kilograms).[5] They are as tall as an average five-year-old boy and weigh as much as a twelve-year-old![6] The larger an animal is, the better it can stand the cold.

KEEPING FEET AND FLIPPERS FROM FREEZING

Emperor penguins are not well-insulated in their flippers and feet, but they keep them from freezing. One way to do this is fine-tuning how much blood flows through their flippers and feet. If they get too cold, blood flow increases. Penguins also cover their feet with the feathers and fat layer of the body to insulate them from freezing winds.[7]

MASTER DIVER

Like its ancestor, emperor penguins are diving birds. But they have taken diving to a new level. They are the most skillful of all diving birds. They can dive more than about 1,800 feet (550 meters) deep and hold their breath longer than twenty minutes.[8] The emperor penguin is an excellent diver for several reasons:

1. Its body has the shape of a torpedo. This makes it easier to dive, gain speed, and save energy.

2. The flippers are modified wings shaped like paddles, which the penguin uses to propel itself underwater.

3. The emperor penguin's blood and muscles hold more oxygen than the blood and muscles of animals that do not dive. Oxygen is the gas in the air that is essential for survival. The more oxygen penguins can store, the longer they can stay underwater feeding or evading a predator, like a leopard seal.[9]

4. Emperor penguins have bones that are solid and heavier than those of flying birds. Having solid, heavy bones helps penguins dive.

If penguins had thin, hollow bones like flying birds, penguins would have a hard time diving. The bones of flying birds usually have air pockets inside, which makes the bird buoyant, or float. Imagine trying to dive with floating devices around your arms. You would have to spend extra energy overcoming your tendency to float.[10]

APRIL: THE MARCH OF THE EMPEROR

By March or April, both male and female penguins have stored as many fat reserves as possible. It is time now to come back to the fast ice to mate, lay an egg, and incubate it for about two months.

Emperor penguins will form a colony or rookery dedicated to hatch the new emperor penguin generation. The rookery is far away

Emperor penguins are skilled underwater swimmers. Their heavy bones help them dive.

from the open sea where predators like leopard seals live, and where the fast ice is thick and solid. For many days and nights, emperor penguins waddle step-by-step or slide on their bellies on the ice to reach this location. Once they have reached the place, emperor penguins mate. The female lays one egg in May or June.[11]

INCUBATING EGGS, THE ANTARCTICA WAY

Emperor penguins do not make a nest to incubate their egg. There are no materials to build a nest with, not even pebbles. Emperor penguins

Emperor penguin courtship involves trumpeting and bonding of pairs.

do not sit on the egg to incubate it. This would instantly freeze the chick growing inside. They place their egg on the top of their feet and tuck it inside the brood pouch. This is an area of soft, smooth skin inside and feathers outside.

The female does not incubate the egg. She has used a great deal of her fat reserves during the march and to produce the egg. She must return to the sea to feed. Before she leaves, she passes the egg to the male. The male alone will incubate the egg while fasting and standing on ice in the middle of the Antarctic winter.[12]

HUDDLING SAVES ENERGY

The males fast for about seventy more days while they incubate their eggs. For the incubation to be successful, the male has to keep the egg at about 96.8°F (36°C).[13] If the egg's temperature varies too much around that number, the incubation will not be successful.

The emperor penguin's body temperature is a careful balance between how much heat the body produces by burning the fat reserves and how much heat he loses to the cold environment. The emperor penguin does not lose too much heat to the environment. His thick layer of fat and tightly packed feathers insulate his body well.

Nevertheless, the temperatures in Antarctica are so much lower than the penguins' body temperature that they still lose heat constantly. They need to burn fat reserves to keep their body temperature constant.

But emperor penguins have limited fat reserves. The male does not have the option to go diving in the ocean again to eat. He has to stand on

Most emperor penguin colonies are usually only a few miles from the sea. The actual distance varies from year to year depending on sea ice conditions. At many of the colonies in the Ross Sea, the distance to the ice edge is less than 3 miles (about 5 kilometers). At the Dumont d'Urville emperor penguin colony, the colony at which the movie *March of the Penguins* was filmed, the distance to open water is often 62 miles (about 100 kilometers). This is specific to this colony, which is an unusual and amazing case.[14]

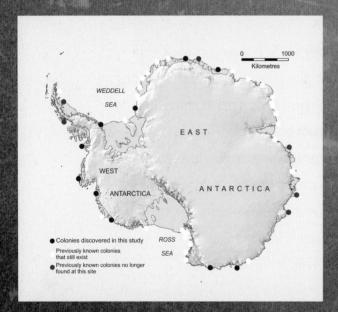

A map of Antarctica showing the location of emperor penguin colonies. In 2009, scientists from the British Antarctic Survey used satellite images to search for the colonies. They could not see penguins, but they could see the brown patches of guano on the ice, which marked the spots.

the ice, often through blizzards while incubating the egg. What he ate in the summer is all he has available. That is why it was so important he had a feast then. If he uses all his fat reserves before the chick hatches, his chances of survival are very low. Emperor penguins survive because they huddle together.

The males form a very tight pack, huddling together in a way similar to what puppies and mice do when they sleep. Huddling works in three ways.[15] First, it protects them more from the cold. The penguins at the edge of the pack have their backs unprotected, but the penguins regularly rotate their positions. Those in the middle take the place of the penguins at the edge, while those at the edge move to the warmer middle. Second, when emperor penguins huddle, they stay very still. This saves energy. Some scientists think they may even take long naps.

Third, huddling warms up the whole pack of penguins. Huddling penguins have created a microenvironment that is warmer than its surroundings. This means they do not have to spend as much energy to keep the body warm. Male emperor penguins that do not huddle spend about 50 percent more energy than huddling emperor penguins. Huddling is one of the most important of the emperor penguins' survival strategies.

AUGUST: THE CHICKS ARE BORN AND MOMS ARE BACK

If the mother has not returned by the time the chick hatches, the father penguin has to feed the chick right after it hatches. If he does not, the chick will die soon. Father penguins feed their chick with a portion of undigested food saved on a crease in their throat. This is a mixture of rich nutrients that keeps the newly hatched penguin alive for one or two days.[16] Hopefully, the mother penguin will be back with more food by the time the chick needs another meal.

SEPTEMBER—NOVEMBER: CHICKS BUILD UP THEIR COLD WEATHER PROTECTION

Newly hatched chicks have a fine grayish feathered coat that does not provide enough protection against the extreme weather. Also, the chicks have yet to build up fat under their skin. When the mother penguin returns, the father transfers the chick to her feet, and she nestles it in her brood pouch. It is her turn to care for the new life. Father penguin has lost almost half the weight he had before the march. He begins to waddle toward the sea to feed.

Around two weeks after hatching, the chicks grow a weatherproof coat and a fat layer that gives them enough protection to step from their mother's feet and onto the ice.[17]

Before long, they will be ready for fledging. In the case of penguins, which do not fly, fledging is not the time when the chicks take their first flight from the nest. Fledging in penguins is when the chicks change into adults, with tightly packed, water-proof feathered coats.[18] Fledging marks the time when the chicks become independent from their parents and are ready to dive.

DECEMBER: ADULTS LEAVE, CHICKS ARE INDEPENDENT, AND THE CYCLE BEGINS AGAIN

After fledging, the adults go back to forage at sea, leaving the chicks on their own. The ice has begun to break and melt and the sea is much closer, sometimes just a few yards (meters) away from the rookery.

The adults molt at this time. They shed the old feathers and replace them with new ones growing underneath. They get a new feathered coat every year to protect them from the freezing temperatures.

An emperor penguin protects its chick from the cold by placing the chick in its brood pouch.

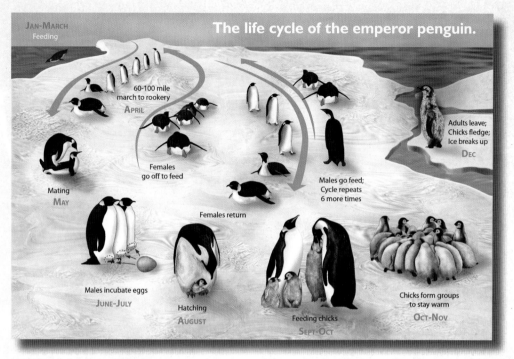

The life cycle of the emperor penguin.

The chicks are now completely independent. They will stay together in small groups and venture into the sea following their instincts to feed and evade predators. When they are three to five years old, they will march through the ice and have chicks of their own, just like their ancestors have done for many generations to survive in Antarctica.

THE MASTERS OF THE ICY WORLDS

The polar bear in the Arctic and the emperor penguin of Antarctica are very different animals that adapted to the coldest places on the planet in their own ways. They show us that life will find a way to survive even in the most extreme places on Earth.

HANDS-ON ACTIVITY
TESTING THE POWER OF BLUBBER

Many Arctic and Antarctic animals have a thick layer of fat, or blubber, under their skin. Try this experiment to find out if blubber can keep you warm.

Materials

You need three ziplock plastic bags (gallon size), one knitted glove, one large can of lard (solid cooking fat), and ice cubes.

Procedure

1. Fill one-third of a plastic bag with water and add about thirty ice cubes.

2. Fill half of a second plastic bag with lard.

3. Place one hand inside the third plastic bag and then into the iced water. Remember how cold it feels.

4. Put the glove on the hand you immersed in the iced water and place it back in the plastic bag. Place it inside the iced water again. How does it feel compared to Step 3?

5. Remove the glove from your hand. Place your bare hand inside the plastic bag and then inside the bag with lard. Now place your hand in the lard inside the iced water. How does it feel compared to Steps 3 and 4?

REACH YOUR CONCLUSIONS

Which is better at keeping your hand warm in iced water: the glove or the lard? Would it be better if you combined the glove and the lard? What other materials do you think would keep you warm? Check it out!

CHAPTER NOTES

Chapter 1. The Icy Worlds: The Arctic and Antarctica

1. Robert Burleigh, *Black Whiteness: Admiral Byrd Alone in the Antarctic* (New York: Atheneum Books for Young Readers, 1998), p. 8. It tells the story of Admiral Richard Byrd, the American explorer who stayed alone on Antarctica for almost six months in 1934.

2. "Facts About Antarctica," *University of Leeds,* n.d., <http://www.ast .leeds.ac.uk/haverah/spaseman/faq.shtml> (August 13, 2010).

3. "Weather in Arctic and Antarctic Regions," *National Geographic Polar Exploration,* 2009, <http://www.nationalgeographic.com/ polarexploration/explore-poles.html> (August 13, 2010).

4. Ibid.

5. Youxue Zhang, "Global Tectonic and Climate Control of Mean Elevation of Continents, and Phanerozoic Sea Level Change," *Earth and Planetary Science Letters,* vol. 237, 2005, p. 528.

6. Elizabeth Manning, "The Long Sleep: Which Animals Hibernate?" *Alaska Fish and Wildlife News,* March 2007, <http://www.wc.adfg.state.ak.us/ index.cfm?adfg=wildlife_news.view_article&articles_id=279&issue_ id=48> (August 13, 2010).

7. Woods Hole Oceanographic Institution, "Compare the Poles: Seasons," *Polar Discovery,* 2006, <http://polardiscovery.whoi.edu/poles/seasons .html> (August 13, 2010).

8. Woods Hole Oceanographic Institution, "Compare the Poles: Weather," *Polar Discovery,* 2006, <http://polardiscovery.whoi.edu/poles/weather .html> (August 13, 2010).

9. National Oceanic Atmospheric Administration (NOAA), "NWS Wind Chill Index," *National Weather Service,* December 17, 2009, <http:// www.nws.noaa.gov/om/windchill/> (July 12, 2010).

Chapter 2. The Polar Bear: The Ice Master of the Arctic

1. C. R. Harington, "The Evolution of Arctic Marine Mammals," *Ecological Applications,* vol. 18, no. 2, supplement, March 2008, pp. S23–25.
2. Ian Stirling, *Polar Bears* (Ann Arbor, Mich.: University of Michigan Press, 1991), p. 147.
3. Harington, pp. S23–25.
4. Joyce A. Quinn, *Arctic and Alpine Biomes* (Westport, Conn.: Greenwood Press, 2008), p. 43.
5. E-mail interview with C. R. Harington, December 2009.
6. Robert Rosing, *The World of the Polar Bear* (Buffalo, N.Y.: Firefly Books, 2006), p. 25.
7. E-mail interview with C. R. Harington, December 2009.
8. Ibid.
9. Ibid.
10. Arnoldus Schytte Blix, *Arctic Animals and Their Adaptations to Life on the Edge* (Trondheim, Norway: Tapir Academic Press, 2005), p. 218.
11. Jane Bosveld, "Top 100 Stories of 2008 #55: Polar Bears (Finally) Make the Endangered Species List," *Discover Magazine,* January 2009, <http://discovermagazine.com/2009/jan/055> (July 12, 2010).
12. Blix, p. 219.
13. Wayne Lynch, "Den Mothers and Their Cubs—Polar Bears," *International Wildlife,* November–December 1994, © 2010, <http://findarticles.com/p/articles/mi_m1170/is_n6_v24/ai_16364226/> (January 4, 2011).
14. Blix, p. 219.

Chapter 3. The Emperor Penguin: The Most Extreme Penguin of Antarctica

1. E-mail interview with Dr. Jessica Meir, December 2009.
2. "Emperor Penguins, Aptenodytes forsteri," *MarineBio.org,* November 8, 2010, <http://marinebio.org/species.asp?id=534> (January 4, 2011).
3. "Antarctic Biology," *Antarctic Resource Page,* n.d., <http://www.antarctica.org.nz/04-biology/index.html> (August 13, 2010).

4. "Adaptations for an Aquatic Environment," InfoBook *Penguins,* 2002, <http://www.seaworld.org/infobooks/penguins/adaptations.html> (February 9, 2011).

5. E-mail interview with Dr. Jessica Meir, December 2009.

6. National Center for Health Statistics in collaboration with the National Center for Chronic Disease Prevention and Health Promotion, "Weight-for-age Percentiles: Boys 2 to 20 Years," *Center for Disease Control (CDC),* May 30, 2000, <http://www.cdc.gov/growthcharts/data/set1/chart03.pdf> (July 12, 2010); "Stature-for-age Percentiles: Boys 2 to 20 Years," <http://www.cdc.gov/growthcharts/data/set1/chart07.pdf> (July 12, 2010).

7. "How Penguins Survive Cold Conditions: Science of the Cold," *Cool Antarctica,* © 2001, <http://www.coolantarctica.com/Antarctica%20 fact%20file/science/cold_penguins.htm> (January 4, 2011).

8. P. J. Ponganis et al., "Returning on Empty: Extreme Blood O2 Depletion Underlies Dive Capacity of Emperor Penguins," *Journal of Experimental Biology,* vol. 210, 2007, pp. 4279–4285.

9. Ibid.

10. Jennifer Hile, "Emperor Penguins: Uniquely Armed for Antarctica," *National Geographic Channel*, March 29, 2004, <http://news .nationalgeographic.com/news/2004/03/0329_040329_TVpenguins .html> (February 9, 2011).

11. "Antarctic Biology."

12. Caroline Gilbert et. al., "Review: Energy Saving Processes in Huddling Emperor Penguins: From Experiments to Theory," *Journal of Experimental Biology,* vol. 211, 2008, pp.1–8.

13. Ibid.

14. E-mail interview with Dr. Jessica Meir, December 2009.

15. "Antarctic Biology."

16. "Antarctic Adaptations," American Museum of Natural History, Rice University, 2002, <http://www.amnh.org/education/resources/rfl/web/ antarctica/s_adaptations.html> (February 9, 2011).

17. Gerald Kooyman et.al., "Penguin Dispersal After Fledging," *Nature,* vol. 383, October 3, 1996, p. 397.

18. E-mail interview with Dr. Jessica Meir, December 2009.

GLOSSARY

ALBEDO • Light reflected by a planet.

ANCESTOR • Distant relation somebody is descended from.

BLUBBER • The insulating fat of ocean mammals.

BUOYANT • Able to float.

CAMOUFLAGE • Concealment of things by disguising them to look like their surroundings.

CARNIVOROUS • Feeding mainly on the flesh of other animals.

FAST ICE • Areas of frozen seawater that grow attached to land.

FROSTBITE • Numbness and tissue death caused by prolonged exposure to freezing conditions.

GLACIER • A large land body of ice and compacted snow.

HIBERNATION • To be in a state similar to sleep for weeks at a time, living off reserves of body fat.

INSULATION • Material that prevents or reduces the passage of heat, electricity, or sound.

MOLTING • To shed feathers, hair, or skin seasonally to allow replacement with new growth.

PACK ICE • Frozen seawater that drifts at sea.

FURTHER READING

Books

Daigle, Evelyne. *The World of Penguins*. Toronto: Tundra Books, 2007.

Dunphy, Madeleine. *Here Is Antarctica*. Berkeley, Calif.: Web of Life Children's Books, 2008.

Rosing, Norbert, and E. Carney. *Face to Face With Polar Bears*. Washington D.C.: National Geographic Children's Books, 2009.

Thornhill, Jan. *This Is My Planet: A Kids' Guide to Global Warming*. Toronto: Maple Tree Press, 2007.

Internet Addresses

National Geographic: Emperor Penguins

<http://animals.nationalgeographic.com/animals/birds/emperor-penguin.html>

Woods Hole Oceanographic Institution: Polar Discovery

<http://polardiscovery.whoi.edu/index.html>

WWF: Polar Bear

<http://wwf.panda.org/what_we_do/where_we_work/arctic/area/species/polarbear/>

Ana María Rodríguez's Homepage

<http://www.anamariarodriguez.com>

INDEX